# Seven Southern Stories

# SEVEN SOUTHERN STORIES: A CANADIAN'S EXPERIENCE OF LIFE IN THE DEEP SOUTH

Amber Shoebridge

Life Rattle Press
Toronto, Canada

Seven Southern Stories: A Canadian's Experience of Life in the Deep South

Copyright ©2020 by Amber Shoebridge

All Rights Reserved.

Published by Life Rattle Press

First Edition

No part of this book may be used or reproduced, stored in a retrieval system, or transmitted, in any form or by any means (including electronic, mechanical, photocopying, recording, or otherwise) without the prior written permission of the publisher, except in the case of brief quotation embodied in reviews.

Life Rattle Press
Toronto, Canada
www.liferattle.ca

ISBN 978-1-989861-13-4

ISSN: 978-1-897161-84-5

Edited by Charleen Sye

Cover, map and photographs by Amber Shoebridge

Dedicated to my family. Especially to my husband Ron, and my children, Lucas and Nicole.

# Map of the Homosassa River

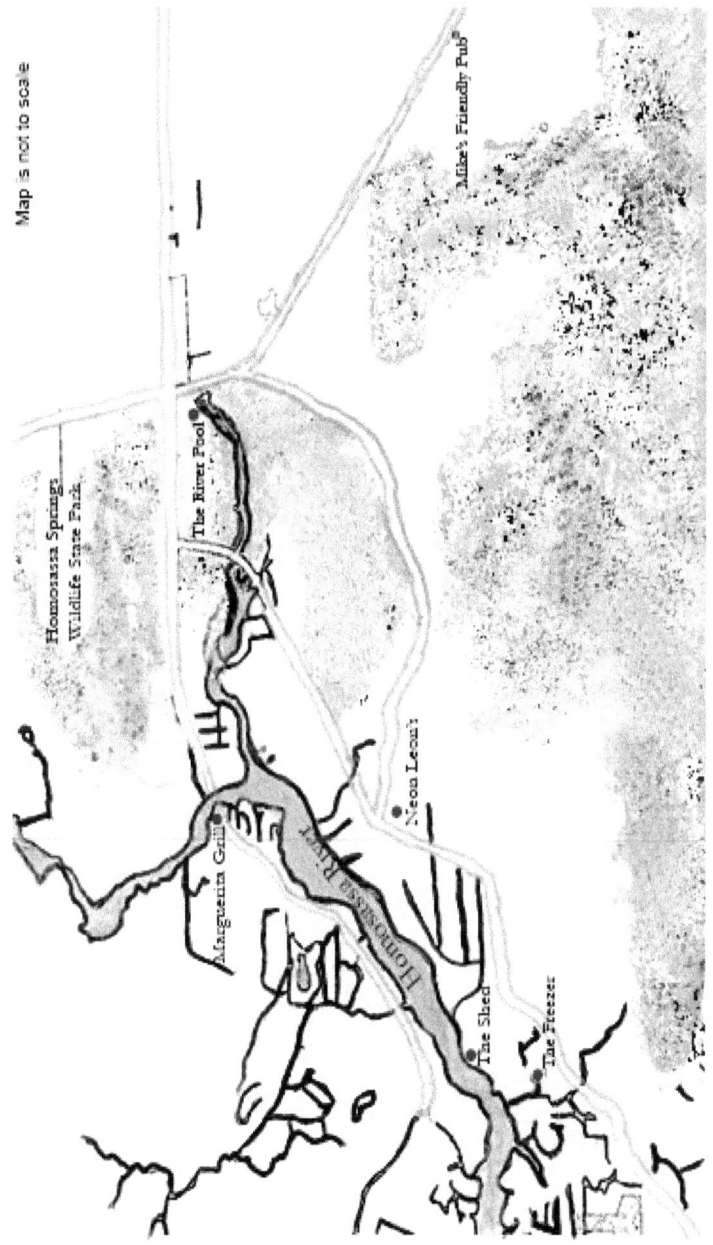

# Preface

My parents are snowbirds and spend roughly five months of the year in Homosassa, Florida. Seven Southern Stories is about some of my experiences with them. My first visit to the small town of Homosassa was in March 2004. This is when these stories begin, other times were over the Christmas holidays a few years later.

The last two stories take place in May 2013 and include my daughter. This is a work of nonfiction, I recreated events, locales, and conversations from memory and journals I wrote at the time. The places are real but some of the names and character qualities of individuals have been changed to maintain their anonymity. This book is by no means a reflection of those businesses or their clientele. What happened on those particular days was my experience and not the experience one can expect if they choose to visit any of those places.

The people of Homosassa that I have met, and associated with over the years have been hospitable and kind. When people refer to "true southern hospitality" I can say I honestly found it here. The places that I have written about range from known tourist hot spots to those that exist off the beaten path.

With time, places and people change, including myself. The Marguerita Grill that I speak of had a fire on July 25, 2011, and has since been rebuilt, it reopened in November of 2017. Neon Leon's sadly closed in 2017 and has been reborn as Mango Tango's Tropical Grill. I have yet to return and visit either.

Many people that I describe in this book have long since retired, moved on, or passed away. Others I decided not to mention, yet.

As I was writing these stories I was asked why? At first, it was just an expansion of my journals as a family memoir, but I decided it was more than that, it is a tribute to my family and the friends who became family in Homosassa. Including restaurants that became a home away from home. There are no judgements just decent food and company.

Canada and the United States are often classified as being similar. That there isn't much difference. That is incorrect. It would be like comparing England to Australia. The language is similar but the landscape and cultures are different, as are some values.

In Canada, we don't carry guns and are more accepting of cultures different from our own. Everyone goes about their business and co-exists without too much issue. There is a police presence but it's nothing like Citrus county.

I want to make clear that the differences do not make either culture or place right or wrong, just different. The stories within these pages are more about my attempt at adjusting and blending into the southern way of life, and creating an extended family with close friends. Enjoy.

# Contents

| | |
|---|---|
| Mike's Friendly Pub | 1 |
| The Shed & The Freezer | 11 |
| Marguerita Grill | 25 |
| The New House | 35 |
| MADD | 45 |
| Neon Leon's | 53 |
| The River Pool | 61 |

# Mike's Friendly Pub

I apply burgundy lip gloss and pucker my lips. Our flight to Tampa, Florida was delayed in Washington, D.C. due to the wind. It's our first time travelling as a family, Ron and I are newlyweds. Barely twenty-five-years-old, we've been married just over a year and have a nine-month-old son, named Lucas. This is our first visit to Homosassa, Florida and it's located an hour's drive north of the Tampa airport.

My Mom and stepdad, Alan, have made this tiny town their winter home for the last two years. On the way to the river house they rented, Mom lets me know they made plans for us this evening. We have just enough time to dump our luggage and change.

Ron and Alan left before us as I needed to feed Lucas. Out of the corner of my eye, I see Mom's reflection in the round bathroom mirror.

"Come on, let's go. There's someone I want you to meet. Her name's Mary, and she's one of the nicest ladies that I've met down here," she says.

"Is she on her way here?" I ask as I comb back my unruly, curly brown hair into a bun. I hear voices in the distance.

"No, we're going for a drink at Mike's Pub. You'll see her there." Mom riffles through her hot pink leather purse for the car keys and heads towards the door. I grab Lucas from the playpen, buckle him in his car seat and follow.

Mom, Lucas, and I pile into the car and head down US 19 Highway through Homosassa. I stare out the window and watch the palm trees pass by in a blur. Mike's Friendly Pub and Deli is located in the strip mall on the corner of Highway 19 and South Oakridge Drive.

We pull into the parking lot filled with rows and rows of motorcycles and a few cars. "Now, don't stare at anyone," Mom instructs as the wind picks up making her voice inaudible.

"What?" I ask as I unhinge the car seat from the back. Mom doesn't hear me and struts towards the pub. I shrug my shoulders and figure if it's important then she would be nagging me by now. I struggle to walk with Lucas' car seat but manage. Mom taps her foot impatiently while holding the door open.

I stop and stare for a moment and read a huge sign taped to the large, picture window. "No colors allowed in the bar. No exceptions."

"Come on, Pokey Joe. You're gonna let all the Freddie flies into the place," Mom says. I walk through the pub door and notice Alan and Ron are seated at the bar.

"Heeey! There they are!" Alan greets us and takes a swig from his pint of beer. He steps off the barstool and grabs a pub-height table large enough for Lucas' car seat to sit on. He drags it closer to the bar where they are seated, helps me unhook Lucas from the car seat, and takes him from me. Lucas' feet flail in excitement to escape the constraints.

"There's my little man. You see this, he's going to be a footballer, look at the size of 'em feet." Alan beams to one of the barmaids. His British accent echoes and fills our end of the bar. He figures with feet as big as Lucas', he's going to be a soccer player. Alan holds him in his arms, swaying him from side-to-side making funny faces. Lucas grabs Alan's face, squeals, and gives gummy kisses.

"Hey, babe. Do you want a drink?" Ron comes up behind me and kisses my cheek, wrapping his arms around my waist and gives me a squeeze. He lets go and grabs my hand, leading me to an empty chair at the bar.

"Sure. What are my options?" I ask, scanning the bar full bikers, locals, and obvious tourists such as ourselves.

The bar is dimly lit, almost lightless. Some of the fluorescent lights flicker on and off while others are burnt out completely. Most of the light streams through the large picture window. The linoleum floor tiles appear to once have been cream coloured, but years of use has a few of them cracked and worn, much like the surrounding wood panel decor that appears to be from the early 1980s.

The long, wooden, U-shaped bar that runs the width of the pub is scratched and in a few places dented. Most people are seated at the other end of the bar and I hear a few playing a game of pool in the back room. The smell of sweat is covered up by the strong smell of rose petal potpourri.

"Uhhh, dunno?" Ron motions to the barmaid leaning on the beer cooler. She takes a swig of her beer and saunters over. Kelly, one of the three barmaids working, is blonde and her hair sits softly on her shoulders. She is roughly six-feet tall and matchstick thin. Her fitted black tank top, faded ripped jeans, and black Doc Marten boots are her uniform.

"Hi, Kelly. What do you have that's not beer?" Ron asks.

"Why? Can't little Miss here handle her beer?" Kelly leans closer to Ron's face.

"She doesn't like it," Ron counters, moving his

face away from hers to take a sip of beer.

"We don't serve 'em fruity drinks here." Kelly sneers and slowly struts across the bar to return to her perch at the cooler.

"I didn't ask for a fruity drink. Do you have vodka or whiskey?" I shot back.

A large, burly man with a snake tattoo proudly displayed on his head and neck slams down his empty beer bottle on the bar. "Kelly, I'm fucking getting old here waiting for ya to serve me. Is that going to happen anytime soon, or what?" he booms, as beads of sweat roll off his forehead, slide down his cheeks, and soaks the neck of his black t-shirt.

Kelly downs the last of her beer, hops off the cooler, and tosses the bottle into the empty case. She grabs a baseball bat, belonging to another barmaid named PJ-according to the paper sign, from beside the cooler, and cracks it on the bar. "Listen, jackass, when I'm ready to serve ya, I'll serve ya, and not a moment sooner. You keep talkin' to me like that you get nuttin', ya hear?" Kelly snarls and spits as she speaks. I'm frozen to my barstool and Ron straightens up ready to grab Lucas and bolt out the door.

"Hey! Whatcha' think you're doin' cussing like that in front of our guests?" A middle-aged, short black-haired woman storms out from the kitchen carrying a large tray of nachos, boiled peanuts, a few grocery store's frozen pizzas, packages of beef jerky, microwave popcorn-still in the bag, and a few pieces of cake. She sets the tray on the bar, takes out a handkerchief, and dabs the sweat from her brow.

"Hi, I'm Mary, it's a pleasure to finally meet y'all." Mary extends her hand and we shake. I stare at the tray. *What kind of pub is this?* I stare at Mom and Alan, and then back at the tray.

The burly man hops off his barstool and comes up from behind Mary, and is about to take some nacho chips, when she turns around and smacks his hand and arm.

"Ohhh no you don't William Levi Johnston. Those are fo' our guests and not fo' the likes of you. Don't you make me call your Mama now, you know I will. Hell, I might even call Big Mike from the back to give ya a whippin' and set ya straight!" Mary continues to hit William with the handkerchief as she speaks. He backs up, step-by-step until he falls back into his barstool.

"Jesus Mary, cut that out! All I was doin' was grabbin' a nacho is all. No need to be so harsh," William says, rubbing his arm.

"Willie, if you want nachos, then you order yo' self some, don't you go lookin' for handouts." Mary rests one hand on her hip while the other is waving her finger inches from his face.

"Last warnin', Willie, or you're barred. Ya hear? I've had enough from you this week. First, you disrespect the place by showin' up in colours, you fo'get to pay yo' tab, then you's cussin', worse! You's cussin' in front of guests, then you try stealin' nachos that aren't meant for the likes of you." Mary glares at Willie as he nods and puts his hands up as if he were under arrest. Mary turns back around.

"I'm so sorry for that little interruption. Willie here musta' left his manners outside," Mary says sweetly, then turns her head, glares at Willie, and raises her eyebrows.

"Uhhh yes'um I'm sorry for cussin' earlier," Willie mumbles bowing his head.

Kelly slams down a bottle of Budweiser in front of Willie and he jumps slightly in his chair. "That'll be a dollar-fifty," Kelly snaps while she chomps on her gum. Willie pulls a few single dollar bills from his wallet and hands them to Kelly. She opens the till and slams it shut, seconds later handing Willie his change.

"Yo Mama has done nothin' but talk about y'all. I feel like I know you already." Mary smiles. Her smile fades as she stares down at the empty bar in front of us.

"It appears Willie isn't the only one who fo'got his manners," Mary yells, turns and glares in Kelly's direction. She shakes her head as she takes the food off of the tray and places it infront of us.

"What can I get y'all ta' drink?" Mary asks.

"Uhh, I'll have a vodka and cranberry please if you have it," I say. "I'll have another Budweiser please, Mary," Ron says, relaxing slightly into his bar stool.

"Ooooh sorry honey, all I have is some wine coolers. Will that do?"

"Yes please, Mary."

"Ohhh yo' Mama was right. You are well mannered," Mary says. "I'll be back in a flash." Mary turns on her heels and grabs our drinks from the far end of the bar. I lean into Ron and half-whisper.

"Remind me never to piss off Mary." Ron laughs. "I don't think you'll ever need reminding," Ron says.

Mary returns with our drinks and places them on the table. "Go on now, eat and drink up. Oh and make sure you try my famous rum cake. I wanna know what you think of it. And you best get on it cause karaoke starts at nine," Mary orders.

"Pardon?" I say, choking on my drink. I stare at Ron and raise my eyebrows. "Karaoke?" I stare at Mom and Alan and they smile.

"Surprise!" Alan says.

"Us? Karaoke?" I sputter.

"Why, yes, child. That's why they brought y'all here," Mary smiles. "Yo' Mama's not half bad singer ya' know," Mary winks and moves to the far end of the bar to take orders.

"Mom sings Karaoke?" I stare at Ron and my mouth hangs open.

"Pick up your jaw dear, or Mary might give you a slap," Ron says as he leans into my ear.

I close my mouth and shake my head. I take large sips of my drink until it empties. The front door constantly opens as patrons continue to pile in, almost all at once, and the bar fills. *Mom and Alan would never in a million years go out at home and sing karaoke. I would never sing karaoke. Mostly because it's embarrassing, and I can't sing. I can't do this, can I?* I raise my hand to grab Mary's attention who is busy opening beers at the end of the bar. "Mary, can I have another drink, please? Actually, can you please bring me two. I'm gonna need it."

# The Shed & The Freezer

The sun bakes my skin. Clouds sporadically block the sun and bring relief. The boat smells old and musty, and is tied to one of the wooden docks at the Marguerita Grill. The smell of dead fish lingers when the wind blows in our direction.

"Come on, love, you better hurry up," Alan orders, throwing the boat into gear.

"Just wait a sec. Here, grab this." Mom throws the rope down to Ron. Grabbing the wooden post for balance, Mom flawlessly steps down onto the bench inside the boat seconds before we pull away from the dock. The boat slowly coasts down the Homosassa River, careful not to create a wake.

The Homosassa River is a no-wake zone. Huge white and orange metal signs hang on large wooden posts beside every other buoy down the river. They indicate the penalties for infractions, including the penalties for injuring a manatee.

The manatees are protected under the Florida Manatee Sanctuary Act of 1978. The minimum fine is five-hundred-dollars and sixty days in jail.

It can be imposed for creating a wake. There are penalties for injuring or killing a manatee. They are a lot more severe. The maximum fine is one-hundred-thousand dollars and one year in prison. A man they nicknamed the "Hanging Judge" I hear handles some of those cases among others in Homosassa. I am told he tends to sentence the maximum penalty.

Mom sits at the very front of the boat and scans for bubbles on the water's surface. Bubbles indicate that a manatee is present just below the water. Mom and Alan decide to take us bar hopping, Florida style: by boat. The Sheriff coasts by us, Alan and Mom wave. A half-mile farther down the river, we pass another Sheriff, Mom and Alan both wave in unison, like robots.

The river is crowded with small fishing and pontoon boats. The water is too shallow for boats that are any larger.

"Doesn't anybody work around here?" I ask Mom. It's 1:00 p.m. on a Wednesday.

Alan lights his pipe and Ron takes the wheel of the boat for a moment. We crawl forward and puffs of blue-white smoke linger behind and disappear.

"Naw, it's not like at home where they work you to death. They finance everything and work as little as possible," Alan explains between puffs.

"Seriously?" I say glancing from Alan to Mom.

"Yep," Mom confirms from her perch at the stern of the boat.

"That's not a bad gig I guess, if you can get it. Not sure I like the idea of being financed to death though, you?" I look at Ron.

Alan takes the wheel back and Ron grabs a beer from the cooler. *Tssst.* The sound of the beer can opening echoes across the river.

*Glug, glug, glug.* Ron wipes his mouth with the side of his hand, leans back and sinks into the boat chair and puts his arm around me. "Nope, but I could get used to this weather." He confesses and takes another gulp of beer. Alan nods his head in agreement. According to the weatherman, it is seventy-five degrees. Alan warned us before we left that the sun's reflection off the water will make feel at least ten degrees warmer.

The boat rounds the bend and we are immediately hit with the sound of a loud bass, and a guitar solo. I look down at Lucas and he doesn't flinch. The motion of the boat keeps him asleep.

As we approach the dock, a large plywood sign with white, spray-painted letters reads: "The Shed."

Rows of wooden docks line the concrete pier. Alan pulls into one of the smaller docks and Mom hops off and ties up the boat. Ron sidesteps the buoy and lands on the dock. I hand Lucas off to him, and Alan grabs my hand to assist me off the boat. I trip on a loose board and he catches me at my waist.

"Easy there," Alan says.

Ron stops walking and looks over his shoulder. "You alright?" He calls back.

"Yeah, I just lost my footing." I look down at my black sandals, now scuffed and pierced from the nail in the loose board. I'm lucky it didn't go into my foot. I gingerly walk the rest of the way down the dock, careful not to stumble on any more loose boards. I grab ahold of a black metal railing and hoist myself up onto the large concrete steps that lead up to the main pier.

The Shed itself is a large wooden bar with faux Hawaiian grass walls and a black metal roof. Plastic blue mesh bar stools line the bar, picnic tables placed two-wide line the pier. The bar has a dance floor that is constructed with wooden two-by-fours screwed together and bolted to the concrete pier. Off to the far right of the pier is a huge dirt parking lot filled with rows and rows of motorcycles, and not a car in sight.

Every twenty-feet hangs a white metal sign with bold black capital letters "No Colors! No Exceptions!"

I nudge Mom in the ribs with my elbow and lean into her ear while Alan scans the bar for a place for us to sit.

"What's no colours?" I inquire. I saw the sign at Mike's pub the day before but forgot to ask. Alan is within earshot and turns around.

"Ah, don't worry about it pet, it's a biker gang thing," Alan explains while he motions us to sit at the picnic table near the bar. Alan sits at the bar and places his straw hat beside him.

I look at Ron and raise my eyebrows. "Gang thing?" I question.

Ron shrugs and puts Lucas on the table in front of me. He takes his seat beside Alan and they order our drinks. I glance down at Lucas who's snoring in his car seat. I shift uneasily. I count the rows upon rows of bikes. There are at least fifty of them, maybe more and I doubt they belong to the same gang.

"Not to worry, Daughter, they're actually really well behaved at this one," Mom says.

Ron appears with our drinks and places them on the table. My vodka and cranberry looks more like pink lemonade. Ron sees the look on my face. "I don't know why it's that colour, I didn't see her make it. Sorry if it's wrong." He kisses my cheek and heads back to the bar with Alan.

I take a sip and choke. The drink is close to straight vodka with a tablespoon of cranberry juice, just enough to turn the vodka pink. *That has to be like four shots, maybe five. I'm going to be drunk after one drink. They would never do this in a million years at home. I'd be lucky if a proper shot was put in my drink.*

"Hey! EHHHHH! Knock it off over there y'all or I'll have to call Sheriff Dawsy." The barmaid's high-pitched voice screeches and echoes off the water. Behind us, an argument between two brawny men heats up as they shout at each other with their faces inches apart. A tall, heavyset, blonde woman pushes her chubby arms between them to pry them apart.

"Well behaved," I mumble under my breath. I roll my eyes and take a small sip of my vodka and cranberry. *Don't worry, Mom says, they're well behaved at this one, she says.* I scan the bar without taking my eyes off anyone. I'm afraid to ask if she has been to others where the bikers weren't well behaved. At home in Canada, the local pub that they visit regularly doubles as a family restaurant, not a biker hang out.

"Jessie, I have a problem startin' over here!" The barmaid shrieks, then snaps her fingers and points in the direction of the fight. A minute passes and a bouncer appears and marches over towards them and breaks them up.

"Don't worry, Daughter, Jessie is pretty good. This should only last about a minute or so." Mom coolly takes another sip of her drink and munches on some pretzels as if she was watching a live version of a soap opera.

Jessie heads over towards Alan, leans in, and asks questions in a hushed tone. Alan talks loud enough so everyone can hear him.

"No, they're both just being jerks, and this one here," Alan points his finger, "he's being the drama queen!" Alan turns back around in his seat and takes a sip of his beer.

"MMMMhmmmm, tha's right," the barmaid confirms.

"Alright y'all, tha's enough or I'll start crackin' heads, ya hear? You," Jessie points to the tall, heavyset blonde woman. "Take one of 'em and leave," Jessie orders. The woman nods and grabs the smaller of the two men. They drunkenly stumble down the pier towards the parking lot.

The larger of the two men steps close to Jessie. Beer spills over the side of his cup. He's completely trashed.

"Yeah, well, fuck you, man! You know shit, ya pussy!" The man spits as he yells. He stumbles to the left, and then to the right, stops and waivers. He drops his beer. It hits the pavement and the red solo cup bounces while beer splatters in every direction. Everyone stares at the empty red plastic cup as it rolls back and forth in the wind.

Jessie grabs the scruff of the man's shirt and

pulls him close enough so their faces are inches apart.

"Sorry man, I just tripped is all. No harm, no foul. I think I need another beer though. Seems I dropped mine." The large man holds up his hands and tries to steady himself while exposing a toothless grin.

"Let's go," says Jessie gruffly, glaring at him. The radio attached to Jessie's belt crackles to life.

"Jessie, we need assistance in section four, over." Jessie grabs the radio off his belt. "Ten-four." Jessie does not hesitate and bolts to a different section of the crowded bar.

"Hey, you! Watch your mouth! There's women and children here!" Alan shouts over his shoulder in the man's direction. Alan's lips, pressed thin, turn a shade of purple. He opens his mouth to speak again but stops and takes a swig of beer instead.

My eyes widen as I stare at Alan, and then at Ron. I give Ron "The Look." *What is he doing? Shut up! They're allowed to carry guns here. Are you nuts!* The image of all the guns that you could buy at Howard's Flea Market from earlier that day enters my mind. Everything from AK-47's to small handguns that could fit into a holster on your leg. They were bought and sold as easy as the mini donuts. Ron knows what I'm thinking and shrugs his shoulders.

The brawny man stumbles towards the bar and grabs a hold of it to steady himself. Ron jumps slightly from his barstool. Alan doesn't move.

"Sorry man, sorry. Didn't realize they 'uz here." The large man puffs out of breath as he attempts to sit on the bar stool. He misses the seat, falls, and hits his jaw on the bar on the way down, and knocks himself out.

Alan glances over his shoulder down at the man lying on the concrete. He shrugs his shoulders, looks over at Mom, and takes the last sip of his beer.

"That'll teach ya for cursin'," Alan mumbles under his breath.

"Ready to go to The Freezer. I'm starving," Mom says cheerily as if nothing happened.

Alan slides off the bar seat, grabs his straw hat off the bar, and places it on his head. He riffles through his pocket, pulls out a ten-dollar bill, and leaves it under the ashtray.

"Hey, Jennifer. Jennifer! You got a man down over here." Alan points towards the concrete. Jennifer walks to our end of the bar, leans over to have a look and continues to make drinks.

"Thanks, Al, I'll take care of it," she says.

Ron looks at me and slides off his bar seat. He grabs Lucas and we head toward the boat. Mom and Alan follow a few feet behind.

"Never again," I mumble under my breath.

We all hop into the boat and idle down the river. Alan drives through a small inlet that is canopied by large trees. For the first time since we've been here, I spot alligators sunning themselves on the shore or gliding in the water.

*Where the hell are they taking us?* I glance up at Ron, and he shifts uneasily. I know he is thinking the same thing as I am. If they wanted to, the alligators could jump into the boat. We learned earlier today from the rangers at the Homosassa Springs Wildlife Park, alligators can jump six-feet high.

Our boat is low to the water, and try as Alan does to steer in the middle, the possibility looms as the shore is close.

Then, out of nowhere, the waterway opens up. Another place lined with docks and boats. The closer we drive, tiki grass and a thatched roof connected to a concrete building come into view. "Another tiki bar," I exhale in relief. *Talk about a place that's off the beaten path.*

Alan finds a place to dock, and this time I manage not to trip getting out of the boat. The place is packed with people. Mom notices people leaving from a nearby table and rushes to claim it. *Seriously! What is wrong with her? I've never seen her do that.* But, just as she does, another group of people try to do the same.

"Sorry, we've got this table," Mom says and smiles. The older couple look deflated until they notice a vacant spot open up along the bar. Like cats on the prowl, they jump into the empty space within seconds.

"We'll go place the order. Do you want shrimp?" Alan asks Mom.

"Yep, full order and," Mom examines the menu, "clam chowder." I look towards Ron and nod.

"Same," I say. I examine the menu and notice how limited it is but the prices are amazing. A full order, if I read it right, is two and a half pounds of shrimp. The cost: seventeen dollars. The clam chowder, three dollars and ninety-five cents. At home, I pay more than that just for a pound of shrimp at home.

I examine the rest of the menu and notice it's mostly various fish and seafood. For those that don't like fish or seafood, choices are limited to a hot dog or steak sandwich, but only on Wednesdays, and if you are desperate, potato chips.

"You'll love the shrimps here," Mom claims while we watch them order our food at the bar.

I'm skeptical. I've eaten more shrimp probably than most people. When I was twelve years old, we visited my grandparents for the Christmas holidays one year. It snowed in Florida that year. We travelled down the gulf coast to Key West and up the Atlantic coast before we travelled home. Every town or city we stopped in I ate shrimp for dinner and lunch, while my Dad ate slices of Key Lime pie. We joked we were connoisseurs by the end of the trip.

"I'll be the judge," I assert. A few moments pass and Ron brings me a bottle of Mike's Hard Lemonade.

"It's all they had," He says apologetically. "It's not like a real bar. They serve bottled beer and Mike's."

"It's fine. I like Mike's," I say with a grin, then take a swig. The people here appear to be normal. Definitely not as drunk as those at The Shed. I peak on Lucas still asleep in his car seat, and despite the noise, he is still fast asleep. It must be the combination of the boat rides and fresh air that have kept him asleep. I am so happy to have a break.

Lucas, at nine-months-old, still has the sleeping pattern of a newborn, up every four to five hours. Maybe with any luck, he'll start sleeping through the night on this trip.

We watch the people and boats go by and drink in silence. Ron has his arm around my neck and I scooch my seat closer to his. I cuddle under his arm and place my hand on his knee. The weather is gorgeous, and the view, a small piece of paradise on this part of the river.

I excuse myself and head towards the washroom. Mom instructs me there are only two, and I might have to wait. I nod and make my way towards the front entrance. As I walk through the plastic cooler strip curtains, I notice workers moving carts of ice and fish.

After my short wait for the washroom, I head back to the table. "You're not going to believe it, this place is an actual fish freezer," I inform Ron while sliding back onto the barstool.

"Really?" Ron says, raising his eyebrows.

"Yep."

"That's pretty neat eh?" Ron says as he takes the shell off a shrimp. "They would never have a place like this at home, the government would never allow it." I nod in agreement. *It would never happen in a million years.*

The food arrived while I was gone and it's piping hot. The shrimp are large and the clam chowder is creamy, made New England style, with the largest chunks of seafood and fish that I've ever seen in a clam chowder soup. Definitely homemade. I try the shrimp, they are seasoned giving them a little heat but not spicy. Mom is right, it is the best shrimp I've ever had. This little pub in the middle of the river is by far my favourite. It's an easy-going, no-frills, good food, feel-good kind of place. Just the way I like it.

# Marguerita Grill

The Marguerita Grill is a pub that sits halfway down the Homosassa River. At happy hour, the parking lot overflows with cars. An old couple leaves the pub with their takeout packages and flop into their car. Mom waits patiently for them to leave. The Jaguar's purr comes to a halt as Mom pulls into the parking space and turns off the engine.

"Come on Daughter, Momma will buy you a margarita."

My stomach growls fiercely. "I'm starving."

"They have the best steak sandwiches in town. They're to die for," Mom declares while taking the keys out of the ignition. We hop out of the car and navigate our way through the uneven gravel parking lot.

As we approach the pub we are greeted by a life-size elephant statue that guards the front doors. A mural of the American flag, a soaring bald eagle, and the burning twin towers are painted from the ground to the roof. "Never Forget" is painted boldly in white on a banner that the eagle holds in its beak.

I shiver. A day I will never forget. The company I worked for, Krombi Group, was in the middle of a finance deal with companies on the thirty-third, fifty-sixth, and seventieth floors.

I sent documents by Fed-Ex to each address the week before September 11, 2001. As I printed the addresses on the Fed-Ex waybills, I fantasized about the views of New York City from those offices. I imagined it to be fantastic, considering my current office was an internal box, painted institutional white without windows. It felt like a prison that permitted casual Fridays.

The papers I sent by Fed-Ex became one of many that littered the sky that day. I prayed they all had a meeting on the thirty-third floor and got out, at least that is what I kept telling myself.

"Dey afta' America. Dey not our problem. Now, go work hard." Mr. Yuang's Chinese accent cuts through my memory. He was my boss, and had little concern for the people in the twin towers, or anyone working in our building. He was more concerned about the finance deal.

That evening, the GO train was empty except for a few people. Most of us were reading a special evening issue of Metro, the free newspaper, it made myself and others sniffle and hold back tears all the way home to Brampton Station. Downtown Toronto was evacuated that morning, as soon as the news of terrorism was confirmed and broadcasted. I wasn't allowed to leave the office. I quit the following week.

The noise of people can be heard from the parking lot. Mom swings open one of the glass double doors while I swing Lucas through, still in his car seat.

The pub itself is dimly lit. My eyes adjust while we wait for the hostess. As she approaches, she looks like an all-American cheerleader, with her high ponytail, flawless makeup, bright red lipstick that matches her two sizes, too small red t-shirt, and Levi's jeans. She motions us to follow her and we make our way towards the booth in the middle of the pub.

Large glass windows show the view of the river, and the houses that line it. Boats idle up and down the river, dodging manatees and occasionally docking at the pub.

"Later we should try and get one of those seats over there," Mom says, pointing towards the stage.

"Why, what's wrong with the booth?"

"Nothing, but the owner puts on a neat show at 8:10 p.m. every night, and it's awesome," says Mom. Alan saunters over with the margaritas.

"Holy crap, Mom, that's huge! Guess we're gonna be here for a while."

Alan laughs at us. "Don't worry pet, Ron's going to drive."

The glass is as large as my head. It holds one litre of a margarita drink and takes up a good portion of the table. I hand Lucas his bottle but he chucks it across the room. *So, we're playing that game tonight, are we?* I think to myself.

I scooch out of the booth, bend down, and pick up the bottle. I feel eyes on me. A stalky, dark haired guy perched beside the end of the bar looks down my top, and I catch him smirking and staring, while talking to customers.

My husband, Ron, strolls over.

"Are you okay?" He asks.

"Yeah, I'm fine, but who's buddy beside the end of the bar?"

"That guy?" Ron motions with his head. I nod. "His name is Ross. He's a bit of a plug," Ron says.

"You don't say." I place Lucas' baby bottle on the table, lean in, put my arms around Ron's neck, and gave him a kiss.

"What's that for?"

"Just 'cause," I say, and glance back at the bar, turning my back to Ross. Hopefully, that gives creep show the message. I glance over my shoulder and catch Ross staring at my ass. I roll my eyes and sit back down into the booth. Ron hands Lucas his bottle, ruffles his hair, and wanders back towards the bar to retake his seat beside Alan.

The door opens and sunlight floods the front end of the bar. Outlines of what appears to be a family come into view.

"Oh my God, they have nerve coming in here," Mom gasps while she stares, ignoring her drink.

The waitress seats them at a table near the front entrance. Most likely for their safety. "Why who are they?" I ask.

"I don't know but they certainly aren't from around here," Mom says.

"How do you know? I mean, really Mom, you wouldn't give them a second look at home. You come here and turn racist on me. What's the matter with you?" I scold.

"Nothing. They're just really outta place here. It makes no difference to me, but folks around here," Mom pauses and glances from side to side. "They don't think like you and me."

"Seriously, Mom, this isn't the sixties. They can't be blaming an entire race for what happens in other countries. An entire race isn't to be blamed. They have to be more educated than that." I take a long sip of my extra-large margarita and stare down the straw.

Mom leans in close to the centre of the table

and speaks in a hushed tone. "Not around here, they aren't. You're talkin' about a place that still recruits people for the Klux Klux Klan in a local newspaper, about twenty miles from here. Think about it. The whole time you've been here, how many people have you seen that aren't white?"

I stop sipping my margarita and think about it. She was right. I haven't seen any other race or culture. Everyone was Caucasian. Goosebumps appear on my arms and I shiver.

The family that walked in a few minutes ago was Pakistani. All the women wore black or navy burkas, long dresses, and long sleeves. It was eighty-five degrees outside even though it was turning dusk.

Lucas laughs at his toys that are hanging from the navy-blue handle of the car seat. He squeals at them, claps his hands and manages to grab his plush bee and pulls the string. He giggles as it vibrates up to the top of the handle.

"Very good, Grandson. Aren't you a smart boy?" Mom coos playfully while she pulls on his chubby cheeks.

A few minutes pass and the pub begins to fill with people from the docks for the dinner hour. The remaining sunlight floods the restaurant again from the parking lot. This time a Sheriff walks through the door. He orders from the bar and takes a seat a few feet from the Pakistani family and scans the patrons at the bar.

Ross serves the food the family ordered, and not one of the waitresses. He stops and jokes with the Sheriff. It's weird seeing police in uniform at a bar. That's not allowed at home unless they're called in. Their food arrives before ours. We were definitely bumped from the cue.

Ross struts over to our table. "Is there anything I can get you ladies?" Again, his gaze is fixated at my chest.

"No, we're good thanks," I say coolly and turn my attention back to Lucas. I jingle his toys and ignore him.

"Great! If you need anything, and I mean anything at all, don't hesitate to call me over." I make the mistake of glancing up at Ross. He winks at me and then struts back to the bar to busy himself.

I roll my eyes. "Creep show," I say flatly and Mom laughs.

A half-hour passes, and the family finishes their dinner, only to return a few minutes later to ask the Sheriff for assistance. Kim, the barmaid, shakes her long blonde hair and throws the bar cloth in disgust on the counter. The cheerleader whispers in Kim's ear. "Really? Someone here slashed all four tires on their minivan?" She glares at everyone at the bar. "Well, I know it wasn't you two," she says while looking at Ron and Alan. They both shrug.

Orders from the other end of the pub come in and Kim pours beer into the pitchers. Bubbles from the draft spill over the side and into the bar tray. I take a large, long sip of my margarita and watch the reactions at the bar. Everyone, seated or standing, is stone-faced. *Seriously! This John Crowe type shit ended decades ago people!* I shake my head.

Our meal that Ron ordered earlier arrives and I test the "American Fries." The owner doesn't recognize the "French," according to the menu. Apparently, he hates the French. His reasoning doesn't make sense to me. They were the ones that supplied Americans with weapons to gain independence from the English.

Lucas is now at the stage of beginning to eat solid foods. I break a fry in half, and blow on it to cool it down. I hand him a piece and he shoves it in his mouth and squishes it between his fingers. His lips pucker from the salt, but he holds his hand out for more. His first taste of "American Fries."

The lights dim further and a projector screen in the middle of the room rolls down. God Save America blares from the speakers. The owner,

Tommy, is a small little Greek man in a tight black t-shirt, faded blue jeans, and black cowboy boots. He struts around the restaurant and onto the dance floor with an oversized American flag.

The bartenders and waitresses scurry around handing out little American flags, hats, and buttons to everyone in the pub. I take mine reluctantly and place it beside Lucas, pretending to be preoccupied with his needs.

The movie starts. It shows footage of the plane crashing into the second twin tower on 9/11 and the local newscasts of that day. My eyes water and I bite down on my tongue. Hard. I do not want to relive that day. I stare at the screen, now trapped into watching it.

The waitresses light sparklers and hand them out to patrons. Lucas' eyes grow large and he stops eating at the sight of them. The movie ends with "We Will Not Forget" in bold, white letters across the black screen. Followed by "We Support Our Troops" and "We Never Leave A Man Behind." Waitresses with plastic buckets and jars move from table to table asking for donations. Heaps of green bills and change fill the jars. Mom pulls out a fiver and puts it in the bucket when the waitress reaches our table.

I raise my eyebrows. "What's that for?"

"The owner is a really nice man. He sends about

fifty-thousand-dollars worth of food and supplies to Afghanistan for the troops, and if someone in town passes away and they have young kids, he helps support them until all the red tape is done for the widows to collect their money."

The people in the small town of Homosassa have good intentions, but it doesn't stop them from making bad judgments.

I sigh. "Only in the South." I take a sip of my never-ending margarita.

"Only in the South," Mom says, grinning, and clinks our margarita glasses.

# The New House

I stumble through the living room in a zombie-like state on the way to the kitchen. My pyjama shirt sticks to my body with sweat and I peel my tongue from the roof of my mouth. Mom is reading the Citrus County Florida newspaper and lounging on the extra-large cream sofa.

"So, how did you sleep Daughter?" Mom asks, not looking up from her newspaper.

Alan smokes his pipe and watches CNN on the television. Puffs of blue-white smoke surround his head then dance towards the screen of the side-door and disappear. Large, primary coloured pieces of my sons' toddler Legos are strewn across the brown shag carpet in the living room.

I map out my route towards the kitchen but step on a few pieces. In the process of keeping my balance, I crack my knee on the corner of the wooden coffee table.

"Ahhh! Mother trucker!" I pause to catch my breath. "Not again!" I bend down and rub the purple bruise on my knee.

Lucas squeals and laughs, clapping his hands.

He crawls to one side of the living room, grabs a Hot Wheels truck, and raises his hand to give it to me. I bend down and kiss his forehead.

"Thanks, baby." I slowly straighten back up and hobble to the kitchen. I bypass the remaining Lego pieces, thankfully, unscathed. I flip on the tea kettle and lean over the counter. Unphased by the Lego landmine I just walked through, Mom grabs her coffee cup, sips, and looks in my direction.

"Not well," I mumble through a yawn. My eyes water and blur my vision. I rub the sandy sleep from the corners and try to focus.

I glance over towards the clock: 9:05 a.m. By Mom's standards, I've slept half the day away.

"I wondered if you'd get up today or not. I hope the noise wasn't too loud," Mom says while she tosses the Citrus County Florida newspaper onto the coffee table and grabs the St. Petersburg Times. She folds a section of the newspaper, grabs a pen off the side-table, and as usual, begins solving the daily crossword puzzle.

"I'm sorry I forgot to tell you that Sheriff Dawsy makes those runs once a week," Mom admits. I sigh and pour the hot water into the waiting teacup on the counter.

3:00 a.m., that same morning:

The bright red numbers from the alarm clock

glare at me. I roll over onto my back to hide from them and stare at the ceiling. The old, cream-coloured ceiling fan, designed in the early 1980s, whirls in a rhythmic hum while the chain bounces off of the attached light.

The nautical-themed sailboat clock hanging on the wall echoes throughout the bedroom. Tic, tic, tic. It's humid. Even though all the windows are open. There is no breeze. The smell of fresh paint hangs in the air. The house is quiet except for the fan, the clock, and the little snores that are coming from my two-year-old son, Lucas. I've barely slept.

Homosassa Springs, Florida is unlike any place we've ever lived. It's too quiet. Mom swore she would always live in the city. I decided being on vacation for a few weeks in a small place is one thing, living in a small place is something entirely different altogether.

The population of Homosassa Springs is roughly twenty-five hundred people. The new house they bought at the end of the tourist season last year backs onto the wildlife reserve full of animals, and dense tropical vegetation. It's also a startling contrast to the city we're originally from, where there are roughly one-hundred and thirty-thousand people in St. Catharines, Ontario, Canada.

It's not as if Homosassa Springs is completely

new to me. I first visited this town two and a half years ago in March 2005. My parents rented a house on the Homosassa River. Boaters, fishermen, dolphins, and various birds are always in the river and it's never completely quiet.

I stare at the shadows that bounce off the ceiling from the reflection of the man-made pond across the road. If you could actually call it a road. It's paved, though barely the width of a car. I hear a rustle in the bushes. According to Alan, wild boar, armadillos, and snakes live behind the house. I see geckos scurry across the window, as their image reflects in the oval white wicker mirror that hangs on the wall. *Well, that explains why I don't even hear crickets.* I take a few deep breaths, close my eyes, and give in to the constant ticks of the clock and drift to sleep.

A loud noise startles me. I glance at the clock: 3:30 a.m. The house vibrates. The noise intensifies and the blinds bounce off the windows. I crane my neck to look out the window without getting out of bed. I see nothing. I look towards the playpen, and Lucas is clutching his teddy-bear, Sam, and sleeping soundly. I slowly roll out of bed and creep toward the window.

Bright lights stream through the blinds and assault my eyes. I stumble backwards, tripping over Lucas' pair of Air Jordan high-top running shoes, and land on the bed. The noise is from a helicopter. It hovers over the retirement village. I kick aside Lucas' little shoes, stand, and pull the blinds slightly to look out the window. Spotlights from the helicopter shift from house to house combing the area. A neighbour's dog from a few houses down howls and barks. Nothing moves in the village. No lights flick on in neighbouring houses, no cars on the roads, no people peering out their windows.

Just me.

I panic. What the hell is going on? The lights continue to bounce from house to house. It's like something you would see in a movie, or on the TV show, Cops. The helicopter lowers closer to the ground. I struggle to see something that might warrant this fly-over.

Nothing.

I remember that Alan said he doesn't lock the house half the time. Earlier that same morning, I gave him shit. It's not like we're at home. Everyone here carries a gun.

"Don't worry, pet," he said. "Citrus County has the lowest crime rate in the state. Nothing happens here." Alan's words echo in my head. *Well, there's a first time for everything. I wonder if they're looking for someone. Great, I bet there's an axe-murderer on the loose.*

I try to quietly open the bedroom door but it sticks, and opens with a small thud. Creeping towards the side door beside my bedroom, I check the deadbolt, and it's locked. I peer out the tiny square windows in the door. The palm trees and tall grass flutter wildly in the wind created by the helicopter.

I navigate my way through the darkness in the living room. The damp carpet squishes between my toes. I hit my knee on the corner of the wooden coffee table and stumble.

"Goddamnit!" I sputter. "Shit!" I hobble towards the kitchen and grab onto the counter for support. Excruciating pain shoots up my leg. I pause for a moment, catch my breath, and wait, hoping I didn't wake anyone.

Staggering through the kitchen, I end up in the den near the back door. I check the door and it's locked. Opposite the back door are a pair of sliding glass doors that lead into the sunroom. The helicopter's lights are streaming through the sunroom. I freeze. I think I see a shadow of a person but I'm not sure. Could this be the person the helicopter is looking for? Paralyzed, I hold my breath.

I stare in the same direction as the helicopter lights revealing the shadow. The branches of a small orange tree whip around wildly in the wind. I forgot Alan mentioned that he planted it yesterday before we arrived. A moment passes, and the helicopter ascends into the sky, turning into nothing more than a flickering red light. The darkness returns as trees and tall grass still to their original positions.

Throwing my hands in the air I hiss, "This is ridiculous."

*I wonder why no one else is up? Especially Mom.* Shrugging my shoulders, I limp back towards my bedroom and gently close the door behind me. Lucas is, miraculously, sleeping soundly with Sam. I creep slowly back into bed. My knee throbs, but after a few moments, I catch myself snoring and slip into a deep sleep.

4:00 a.m.

I awake to the squeal of tires weaving around the retirement village. A car without a muffler accelerates and brakes every few feet. Something hits my window. I jump from the noise and hop out of bed. A dark-coloured, beat-up, rusted-out Monte Carlo, circa the 1980s, is speeding and stopping. The driver is throwing newspapers out of the driver's side window, up and over the car. You have got to be kidding me. That's the paperboy! Shaking my head, I crawl back into bed, grab my pillow, and fluff and pound it in frustration. I glance one more time in Lucas' direction and throw my head back onto the pillow. I take a few deep breaths as the park becomes silent again and doze off to sleep once more.

5:00 a.m.

A high-pitched screech echoes in the house. I awake with a jolt. My eyes widen as I listen again. Is that a cry? I look over towards the wall and notice the empty playpen. Is that Lucas? Flinging the blankets off of my bed, I whip open the bedroom door. Nobody is in the living room. I continue through to the kitchen as the screeching becomes louder. I reach the den and look out into the sunroom where Alan is bouncing Lucas up and down in his arms.

"Yeah, you see that, buddy?" Alan points at something outside the sunroom.

"That's called a peacock. He's noisy, isn't he?" Lucas grabs Alan's face and gives him kisses. I breathe a sigh of relief. A large peacock endowed with indigo feathers spans his wings and struts in the backyard. Two brown females are nearby, pecking at the ground for bugs or worms. It's mating season. I roll my eyes.

"If he doesn't be quiet, that bird's going to be dinner," I say flatly. "Do you want something to eat, buddy?" I ask Lucas. Alan turns in my direction with Lucas resting on his hip.

"It's alright, pet, I'll feed him. You go back to bed," Alan says.

"Are you sure?"

Alan nods, "Go on."

A yawn escapes as I shuffle through the house back to my bedroom. I flop back into bed as the peacock continues to screech. I bury myself under the blankets as he screeches again, and I cringe. I grab the extra pillow, and smother it over my head. Exhaustion takes over, and I drift back to sleep.

# MADD

I hear ice cubes noisily drop to the bottom of a glass. Mom is making drinks. "Amber Dawn! Jersey Jim is here!" Mom hollers from the kitchen.

I finish wrapping a Christmas gift and leave it on the turquoise, seashell print comforter on the bed. My feet squish on the damp brown shag carpet and I head to the living room through my bedroom door.

Jim arrived from Cape May, New Jersey in his new, black 1967 Corvette. He is one of three men that Alan has met since my parent's arrival, and they are all named Jim. So as a means to differentiate between them, Alan includes the places they are from.

Alan was already out the door, admiring the stealthy beast. Mom leaves the drinks on the kitchen counter. I grab one for Jimmy and hand it to him as he walks through the side door with Alan coming up behind. We all take a seat in the living room.

"What service. I wish I had this at home," Jimmy confesses with a smile.

"Yeah, yeah, that's what Ron says, too," I tease and wink at Jimmy. "So, what's happening?"

"You know, not too much. The drive down was great. I was able to put the top down once I crossed the state line. Got a little burnt, I think." Jimmy says as he rubs his sunburned head.

"Awe, you look cute with a little pink melon," I quip.

Jimmy is six-foot-three and has a muscular build, steel blue eyes, and a bald head. His white mustache is the only telling sign of his age.

"How's business? Did you get zinged by the IRS this year? Alan did," I say, taking a sip of my vodka and iced tea. Jimmy owns a landscape business in Cape May and is only able to spend a few months of the winter in Florida. We only get to visit during the holidays.

"Nah, they don't bother with me," Jimmy confesses, sipping his glass of scotch.

"Well, no fricken' wonder. They probably see your income tax report and don't even look at it," Alan jests.

I give a puzzled look. "Why wouldn't they look at it?"

"Jimmy here is a retired navy seal, they probably have a special pile for guys like him," Alan explains smiling and Jimmy laughs.

"Yeah, you're probably right." I joke. "They'd be afraid you'd track them down if they charged you. So, when's Anna May coming down?" Anna May is Jimmy's girlfriend.

"Well, she's kinda doin' her own thing, and I'm not good company this time a' year," Jimmy admits as he swirls the melting ice around in his glass and takes another sip.

"Why? Is she sick of your mug 'cause the only cookin' you like is from a barbeque? I bet you told her you planned on barbequing the turkey and she turned you down," I joke. "Why don't you have Christmas dinner with us? At least you won't be alone for Christmas."

Lucas, my three-year-old son, runs through the kitchen to the living room, grabs one of his toy hockey players, and runs back towards the sunroom.

"Nah, that's okay, I'm good on my own," Jimmy mutters. His smile is frozen and forced.

"No way, there is no way you're spending Christmas on your own. It's the best season of the year," I insist.

"Amber Dawn, that's enough," Mom snaps. I raise my eyebrows.

"What? Why? Is Jimmy not allowed for dinner? I'm only teasing him about the barbeque thing, he knows that. I didn't think I was that offensive, was I?" I turn to Jimmy.

"Nah, it's alright, Cathy, she should probably know. About five years ago, my daughter, who would be about your age, was killed by a drunk driver after Christmas shopping."

I blink and stare at Jimmy. "What! You're serious?" I look at everyone in the room. Mom is glaring at me. "Jimmy, I'm so sorry… I…" my voice trails off.

"Well, you know, it is what it is. You had no way of knowing that's why I hate Christmas. I mean, I look at you, and you have such a nice little family, and think, well, you know, she's missed out on that part of her life," Jimmy says. A tear slips down his cheek. He quickly wipes it with his hand.

"Well, I didn't know her, Jimmy, but I don't think she'd want you to be by yourself for Christmas. If you change your mind and want to temporarily forget what happened, you can still come for dinner."

"Thanks, but I'll be fine," Jimmy says. He gulps down the rest of his scotch. "I should get going so you guys can begin celebrating." He pulls the keys from his pocket, gives an awkward wave goodbye, and escapes out the side-door in the living room. I sigh and rub my hands over my face. Mom grabs my glass and refills it.

"I'll have a double, please." A few moments pass in silence. I sigh, grab my glass, and head back to the bedroom to wrap more gifts.

Christmas day, around dinner time:

I cook Christmas dinner for everyone and I grab an extra plate out of the cupboard.

"Who's that for?" Alan asks.

"Jimmy. I'm going to make one up and walk it over."

"Oh, I don't know. He wants to be alone, pet. He's probably already pretty drunk. Let the man be."

"There's irony," I roll my eyes. "He still has to eat something," I say as I wrap the dinner plate.

I step out the front porch and turn left down the single, paved road. The retirement village consists of mobile homes that are mostly white, cream, or beige and occasionally a grey one. Almost all of them have screened-in porches or sunrooms.

At the corner of the street, I turn right. Jimmy's house is the fourth one in from the corner. I head up the driveway and see that all the lights are off except for the glow of the flickering television. I open the door to the enclosed front porch and knock on the door. Jimmy doesn't answer.

"Jimmy, it's Amber. I have some dinner here for you. I'll just leave it on the table for you."

I put the plate on the patio table on the porch, turn, and walk down the stairs to the end of the driveway. A little MADD red ribbon flickers in the wind on the black Corvette's antennae. I sigh. I'm about three houses away and hear the squeaky front door of Jimmy's house open and then close. I smile. I knew he would eat.

New Year's Day:

Jimmy stops by to return Mom's plate. "You are one stubborn woman, you know that? You don't take no for an answer, do you?"

"Nah, are you kidding? I made way too much food. I could have fed the whole park."

Jimmy sits at the patio table and Alan pours him a beer. "I have great news," Jimmy says with a smile.

"You won the lottery and you've come to share," I say sarcastically.

"You can say that, my daughter's pregnant. They told her she couldn't even have kids and bam! She calls this mornin' and says she's pregnant." Jimmy beams. He is so excited he's jumping around like a kid on a sugar high in the living room.

"Wait, I thought…" my voice trails off.

"No, no, I have another daughter," Jimmy says.

"That's awesome Jimmy, I had no idea. When's she due?"

"Sometime at the end of May." Jimmy can't stop smiling.

"Well, that calls for a celebration!" Mom says as she hops off the patio chair and disappears into the kitchen. She reappears seconds later with a tray of champagne and glasses. I grab the glasses off the tray and place a few on the table. Ron grabs the Champagne. I follow Ron out the door to the back of the house. Ron pops the cork and it flies into the sky and lands somewhere in the bushes.

"Good one," I say with a smile and pat his butt. We walk back inside and Ron begins pouring as I hand everyone a glass.

"You know, a little one will change everything. Trust me, I know," Alan says, referring to Lucas.

"Nah, I'll still hate Christmas. A little person won't change that." Jimmy maintains.

I smile behind my glass of champagne. I know different.

Christmas Eve, two years later:

It's Mom's turn to host us for Christmas, and Jimmy hasn't arrived yet.

"Hey, Mom, when are you expecting Jersey Jim? He's usually here by now," I say as I move the sheer curtain to peek out the window.

"He's not coming until New Year's," Mom says as she continues writing on her crossword puzzle without looking up. Frustrated she tosses her glasses on the coffee table and puts aside the crossword for Alan to continue solving later.

"How come?" I say and flop down on the couch beside her.

"Not sure. He emailed Alan last night to let us know not to expect him," Mom says. She pulls out an envelope from the basket that sits on the coffee table.

"I forgot to tell you this came in the mail for you today." Mom hands me an envelope. Mail? I never receive mail unless it's a parcel I ordered. Puzzled I open it and see it's a Christmas card.

*Dear Amber and Family,*

*I would like to thank you for all of your patience and kindness you have shown me through the years. It's really appreciated. I know I can be a stubborn mule set in my ways and I don't do this often but you were right. I can still remember my daughter Rachel and enjoy Christmas with little Ryan. Thanks for setting me straight. Have a wonderful Christmas and I'll see you guys New Year's Eve.*

*Jersey Jim.*

I smile. "It's Christmas Eve, and it's time for drinks Mom." I place the card with the others on the side table and head into the kitchen.

# Neon Leon's

The sun sets in Old Homosassa. Palm trees line the streets and canopy the road. Mom pulls the car up into one of the parking spaces in front of Neon Leon's Zydeco Steak House. The sign is a flashback from the 1980s. The extra-large tube letters flicker and glow in neon green.

The restaurant is an old, converted ranch style house. Faux rock covers halfway up the building. The patio is a sandpit with a few red-stained picnic tables with beer umbrellas set in the centre.

Mom has bragged about this little restaurant for weeks before we arrived today. The bass player from Lynyrd Skynyrd, Leon Wilkeson, is the owner. His son, Lee, and his nephew, Mitch, run the place.

Nicole, my three-year-old daughter, and I hold hands as we stroll up the sidewalk. Mom and my nine-year-old son, Lucas, follow behind me. We meet up with Ron and Alan as they came in a separate car from a pub named Gator Cove. They are patiently waiting by the entrance.

We enter the restaurant through an aluminum screen door. It creaks as it slams shut. The smell of grease slaps my face, and my stomach growls.

The music is loud. A three-man band plays classic rock music from the 1970s. The band consists of a man, his wife, and a computer. The computer plays back-up to his guitar. His wife plays the cymbal. The restaurant is half-empty and full of locals dressed in flip flops and shorts.

Mom leads us to a table in front of the stage. My red high heel sticks in between the joints of the old, dusty wooden floor and I stumble forward. Ron grabs my arm and waist to steady me. I look around to see if anyone noticed. Everyone looks in our direction and my face turns crimson.

"You alright?" Ron asks concerned.

"Yeah, I'm just a clutz," I say as I check to see if I ruined my new red leather high heel shoes.

"It's pretty bad when we need to cut you off before you get started," Ron winks at me, and my jaw drops slightly as I gasp.

"Jerk!" I playfully punch Ron in the arm and he laughs.

I ease along the wooden ramp on the balls of my feet and we make our way to our seats. The brown Formica table is covered with a vinyl, green plaid tablecloth. We sink into the comfortable brown vinyl stacking chairs. Wood panelling covers the walls. The beams, painted an off-white, are peeling and cracking from the humidity. The ceiling fans hum and squeal in protest.

My porcelain skin glows under the dim lights and screams, "You're a tourist!" Mom said this restaurant was a five star. I scan around the room and sigh.

Noticing the expression on my face, Alan murmurs, "Don't be so quick to judge. Trust me, the food is good."

The band takes a break and we order drinks. The menu: hamburgers, hotdogs, steak, chicken, grouper, tilapia, frog's legs, crab cakes, oysters, jambalaya, gator tail, catfish, gumbos, and creoles of every kind. All authentic southern Louisiana-style food. I lean over the table towards Mom.

"How on Earth does a rock star open a restaurant here in Homosassa?" I whisper. Mom leans in to talk to me.

"Well, a lot of people from back then, in the 1960s and 1970s from Louisiana would make this a vacation destination like the people back home make up north a destination. Same kinda thing."

"Vacation here? The weather is virtually the same." I stare narrowly down at her.

"A lot of people had cottages here, some still do." Mom puts down the menu on the table.

"I think I'm ordering the crab cakes. I've been dreaming about them for weeks," Mom announces and sips her drink.

The band sets up and the guitar player tunes his guitar. I watch his wife click the mouse through hundreds of musical files before settling on the one she wants to play. We place our orders with our waitress.

"Well looky here, where y'all from?" The guitar player asks.

"Canada," Mom pipes up.

"Not you, sweetheart, you're here all the time. I was askin' where they're from. This must be yo' family?" he asks Mom.

"This is my daughter, her husband, my grandson Lucas, and my granddaughter Nicole," Mom beams.

"Uh-huh, y'all enjoy the weather, ya' hear?" Says the guitar player.

"Will do," I say and take a sip of my drink. It's supposed to be vodka and cranberry. The cranberry looks more like pink lemonade. I try not to make a face as I drink it.

"Do you want that in a tall glass, Daughter?" Mom asks.

"A what?" I ask.

"Do you want more cranberry juice so you can actually drink it without taking baby sips?"

"Yes, please." Thank God, I thought I was going to have to choke down the drink. It's been a while since I've had drinks like this and I was completely out of practice as to how to handle them.

"Melissa, honey, can you water down this Northerner's drink with more mix, please? I'd like to get started." The guitar player points me out to the waitress at the bar.

"Get started, huh? I'm confused. Why does my drink have anything to do with getting started?" I look straight at Mom. Her face is expressionless.

"This is an interactive show. You'll have so much fun," Mom says as she claps her hands.

"Interactive? Me? Uh, no, not me." My ears burn and I can feel my face turning a bright shade of pink.

"Heeelllo everybody, my name is Billy Bob and no, I'm not related to the famous actor Billy Bob Thornton, although I've been told I look like him, but if you like you can throw your money at me like people do at Mr. Thornton, I won't mind a bit. The tip jar is right here and I'll even get y'all started an' donate the first dollar to myself. It's quick an' easy, much like myself. Don't be shy cause a mans gotta eat."

Billy Bob is a chubby, sixty-year-old man whose hair is balding in the front and has a longpony tail in the back. He wears wire-rimmed glasses, khaki golf shirt, and white bermuda shorts and running shoes.

"How ol' are ya sweetheart?" Billy Bob asks Nicole.

"Fweee," Nicole responds.

"Would you like to come up here and play the tambourine?" Billy Bob asks.

"Yees, pweeease." Nicole claps her hands, jumps down from her chair, and hops onto the stage.

"Here, put these on. Now, you can't be a rockstar without a cool pair a' shades," Billy Bob informs her.

The sunglasses are gigantic and they force Nicole to look up at the lights so they can rest on her face without sliding off her nose. The first few chords of Sweet Home Alabama play and Nicole plays the tambourine while swaying her tiny hips side-to-side. Every now and then she twirls, ballooning her leopard print dress.

A steady flow of people drop money into the tip jar, and from what I gather it looks like a good start to the night. The song ends and Billy Bob adjusts his guitar.

"Alright, everyone, let's give it up for my girl, Nicole!" he shouts.

"Now, darlin', has your granny been havin' you practicin'?" He bends down to talk to her.

"No. I dud it myyyyself," Nicole beams. Her hands resting a-matter of-factly on her hips.

"Well, I think as a musician, my girl here, should be paid! What do y'all think about that?" Billy Bob hollers. Hoots and cheers erupt from the tiny restaurant, now crowded. He reaches into the overflowing tip jar and pulls out a dollar bill and places it into Nicole's hand.

A wide smile appears across her face"Look Mummy, a penny!" arms in the air, with the crumpled dollar bill peeking from her tiny hand, Nicole leaps off the stage and runs up to show me.

# The River Pool

Detroit Jimmy grabs a hotdog off the barbeque and places it on a grilled bun. He motions his head towards my nine-year-old son, Lucas. "I love this age where they still have this naivety about them," Jimmy murmurs.

The palm trees slowly flutter about in the wind. The glaring sun sneaks from behind the clouds and warms the air. The average temperature of the Homosassa River is seventy-two degrees as it is naturally warmed by the hot springs. Today, the river is calm and feels warmer than usual. Mom and Alan sun themselves on lounge chairs while my three-year-old daughter, Nicole, plays with toys in the sand.

I grab hotdogs for Lucas and myself from the barbeque and saunter back over towards the patio table to sit down. "Watch this." Jimmy whispers and winks at me from across the table. He fishes in his pocket and pulls out a shiny blue, iridescent stone from his pocket, the kind that you buy for vases from the dollar store.

"Hey, Lucas, do you know what this is?" Jimmy asks.

"It looks like a rock of some kind," Lucas guesses between bites.

"You're right, but you know how this rock is made?"

"Nope," Lucas shrugs uninterested and grabs some potato chips from the bag and tosses a handful on his plate. He starts chomping on them.

"Do you want to know a magical secret?" Jimmy whispers. He lowers his head closer towards Lucas and looks around from left to right.

"Yeah right, magical secret," Lucas scoffs and takes a large gulp of his A&W root beer. He lets out a small belch and excuses himself.

"No, I'm serious here, goalie to goalie. I will tell ya how it's made. My granddaughters are the only other ones who know how this secret happens, but I was thinkin'. You should be a part of the secret. Do ya wanna know?" Jimmy stares at Lucas squarely in the eyes. Lucas nods his head and inhales the other half of his hotdog. Ketchup slides down his cheek. Jimmy gets up and faces the river.

"You see my blue light up there?" Jimmy points high up into the banana tree that leans against the light post. He turns back and sees Lucas nod. "I have to leave it on at night during a rainstorm and then something magical happens, lightning strikes down into my river pool and then when I wake up the next day I find all of these little rocks sitting in the sand on the bottom of the pool. Cool, huh?" Jimmy glances over his shoulder towards Lucas to gauge if he's bought the story.

"Yeah, right," Lucas shrugs off the explanation. He wipes the ketchup off his face with the back of his hand only to smear it further across his cheek.

I tighten my lips, sigh, look away and shake my head in embarrassment. "Really?" says Lucas and his eyes widen.

"I bet after lunch, if you dive down into the water you'll probably see a whole bunch of these since it stormed last night. I collect them you know?" Jimmy turns back around, grabs a beer from the cooler, and opens it. "I'll tell you what Lucas, you can keep what you find."

*Psssscha.* The sound of the beer can opening echoes across the yard. Beer foams over and slides down the can, over Jimmy's hand and splatters onto the grey, diamond-shaped patio stones.

"I better get some water and clean this up or we'll be fightin' off the fire ants from hell," Jimmy announces and heads to the side of the house to fetch the hose.

We all nod in agreement. Fire ants are the worst. For such small bugs their sting is brutal, and at times almost unbearable. I remember the first time I was bit, I screamed it was so painful, and my big toe was swollen for a week.

"That sounds pretty cool eh buddy, don't you think? You get to keep what you find." I gaze towards the water and take a sip of lemonade.

"Mom, can I go swimming now? I'm done." Lucas wipes his mouth, crumples his paper napkin and tosses it on the paper plate. Jimmy returns, sprays down the spilt beer, drops the hose, and flops back down into the patio chair at the table.

"Sure, buddy, just be careful." I grab my fork and poke at my warm potato salad. Jimmy winks at me from across the table reassuringly and I smile. He was right. There still is a little magic to be had at this age.

Lucas heads into the change house to put on his swim trunks. Jimmy bolts from the table towards the river pool and throws handfuls of the blue rocks from his pockets into the water. The door to the change house slams.

Jimmy jogs toward the dock, boards his kayak, and paddles down the river under the cover of tall grass and palm trees. I pretend to read my Home and Garden magazine while eating the warm potato salad. The click, click, click of Lucas' flip flops on the patio stones echoes and becomes louder as he approaches the patio table.

"Hey, Mom, where's Jimmy?" Lucas asks while scanning the yard.

"Oh, he went kayaking buddy, but he'll be back shortly," I say while I flip the page of my magazine pretending to read the article.

Lucas shrugs and heads toward the ladder to the green waterslide. He climbs to the top, stands, and looks up and down the river. He slowly bends over, grabs the handles, sits, and throttles himself down the slide plunging into the river pool. I grab my lemonade and sit down beside Alan on the vacant, canary yellow lounge chair that sits across from the pool.

"Alan, how long have you known Detroit Jimmy?" I ask.

Alan takes out his shiny gold and black package of Captain Black tobacco and fills his pipe. "Well, Detroit Jimmy was the first guy I met here at the pub. He can be an arrogant son-of-a-bitch when he wants to be, but he's not stupid, so I like him."

Alan raises the pipe to his mouth and lights it. Puffs of blue-white smoke billow and hang in the humid air. "You know, Jimmy played for the Kitchener Rangers back in the sixties. That was the farm team for the New York Rangers. They didn't keep back-up goalies on the bench like they do now. So, he's spent a lotta' time in Canada."

"He spent time in Kitchener? Poor guy," I say. Kitchener is where we currently spend most of the hockey season with Lucas' team. Kitchener has four teams to our one. Every other weekend so far this winter has been spent there, and I hate the drive.

Alan takes a few puffs of his pipe. "So, he's not stupid. I mean, look at this place. Some real thought was put into this. I mean, it's not like he couldn't afford a swimming pool." Alan motions his head towards the river pool.

"He's really an educated guy. He used to write commercials and TV shows and stuff for the major networks. Every other week he'd fly from Detroit to California." Alan shakes his head and takes a few more puffs of his pipe.

"Crazy bastard. He's such a great guy. He'd do anything for ya," Alan murmurs.

Jimmy docks his kayak and steadily hops out. He leans over and hoists the kayak effortlessly above his head in one motion. His six-foot-five frame easily puts the kayak in the holders bolted to the fence. If it wasn't for his salt-and-pepper hair and beard, and the beginnings of a beer belly, you'd never guess he was getting close to being seventy-years-old. He strolls over to the patio table and plops down into the patio chair.

"So, Luke, how you makin' out buddy?" Jimmy calls in the direction of the pool.

"Gooood, I'm finding all kinds of 'em!" Lucas hollers splashing around the pool.

I rise from the yellow lounge chair and sit back down at the patio table. *Pssscha*. Jimmy cracks open another can of Coors Light. Sweat slides down his forehead and cheeks, and drips onto his grey, sweat-stained t-shirt.

"The other beer was a decoy, this one is earned," Jimmy declares and I smile. Lucas bolts from the river pool across the hot sand with a handful of shiny, blue, glass rocks.

"Look at these!" Lucas grins.

Nicole stops playing in the sand and comes over to the table and marvels, "Ohhhh, they're pretty."

Lucas contemplates the pile on the table and separates the glass rocks. "You can have these ones," Lucas continues to examine the pile and is please with his selection. "Okay?" he looks down at Nicole.

Nicole nods, wide-eyed, and smiles. "Thaaank-you." She gives Lucas a hug while clutching the blue stones.

Lucas bends down to her eye level. "Do you know how they're made?"

Nicole shakes her head. Lucas grabs her hand

and drags her across the lawn to the same banana tree Jimmy was near earlier. He points to the lamp post that sits near the edge of the river pool.

"Do you see Jimmy's blue light up there?" Nicole nods. "Well, you see, when there's a storm like we had last night…"

Without taking my eyes off the kids, I ask Jimmy, "How did you come up with the design of the river pool?"

"Hey Mom, can we go back into the pool?" Lucas interrupts.

I nod. "Just pay attention to your sister a little, okay?"

Lucas agrees and helps her with the lifejacket, but struggles with the buckle. "Go see Mom."

Nicole trots over. I secure the lifejacket and kiss her on the forehead. "Go have fun. Lucas, be careful." I give Lucas a look and he gives me a thumbs up.

Jimmy smiles as he watches the kids play in the pool. I imagine he wishes his granddaughters lived closer than Detroit. Jimmy dives into the potato chips in the bowl on the table and washes them down with a swig of beer while contemplating my question. "Well, back in the eighties, I dug a huge trench on this property in the shape of a swimming pool and lined the inside walls with concrete and rocks. I attached a screened gate at the end there, closest to the river so none of the wildlife could come in. On one of my flights from L.A. to Detroit, I had this idea of utilizing the river to create a pool. It's a pool I never had to fill or clean with chemicals. Hence the beginning of my oasis, my very own blue lagoon," Jimmy opens his arms and scans the yard from left to right.

I sip my lemonade processing the brilliant creation. Jimmy leans over and grabs the vodka from the cooler and puts some in my drink. "Live a little sweetheart, you're on holidays. Cheers," Jimmy urges and raises his glass. I smile and clink my glass with Jimmy's.

"Mom, Mooom, MOOOOOOM!" Water drips from Lucas' diving mask and slides down his face. He slowly wades through the pool towards the rocky steps and climbs them, Nicole tags behind.

"Yeah, buddy, what's up?" I move from my patio chair and trudge through the scorching white sand towards him. I bolt towards the rocky steps and plunge my feet into the cool water.

"Look at 'em all. And I also found this." Lucas takes a large, round, rusted metal object, a little larger than a marble, and holds it up to the sun.

"Yeeeah, buddy, I don't think that was created by the storm. Where exactly did you find that?" I ask.

"Over there, by the gate." Lucas points by the

steep rocks that are connected to the gate that keeps the wildlife out of Jimmy's pool.

"Jimmy, Jim!" I yell towards the patio area. "I think you better have a look at this. It seems your river pool is magical in more ways than one." I climb the stairs with the round metal ball in my hand and bolt across the scorching sand towards the patio area.

"Why, what did you find? Gold, I hope," Jimmy jokes, grinning and sipping his beer.

I laugh, slide on my sandals, and stand beside him. I place the round ball on the table. Jimmy grabs the ball in his large meaty hands and examines it.

"Jimmy, do you know what that is? I am willing to bet it's a musket bullet," I speculate.

"You think so?"

"Yeah, you see them all the time in Niagara, the War of 1812 and all. Other than the rust, that looks and feels exactly like one. The Civil War didn't happen this far down, did it?" I inquire. Lucas and Nicole grab towels and sit on the stone bench at the patio table to dry off.

"Sure did. Old Man Yulee had his mansion and mill burnt down by the Northerners. They did have a fight on the river. It could be from that," Jimmy explains.

"Or it could be from some poor sucker who

was fightin' off a gator and lost," Alan responds sarcastically. We all laugh.

"Who's Old Man Yulee?" Lucas asks.

"He was a rich mill owner who owned all the land from Gainesville to here," Jimmy declares.

"Gainesville? That's like, two and half hours from here, by car," I add and raise my eyebrows in disbelief. *Wow, I can't imagine how one person could own that much land, especially back then.*

"Well, Luke, it looks like you got yourself a treasure from this holiday. You can keep the bullet," Jimmy says, placing it back in Lucas' hands.

"Really? I can?" Lucas marvels at the prospect and Jimmy nods. "Coooool! Wait 'til I phone Dad and tell him." Ron is a few days away from arriving for the Christmas holidays, and he's never going to believe it.

# Acknowledgements

I would like to thank all of the Professors in the Professional Writing and Communication program, at the University of Toronto Mississauga. Their encouragement, support, and wealth of knowledge is greatly appreciated. Especially Professors Laurel Waterman, Robert Price, John Currie, Alessandro Delfanti, and Rahul Sethi. This wonderful journey would not have been possible without you.

This book would not have been possible without the WRI420 Making a Book course, created by the programs Director, Professor Guy Allen. What you do for your students and this program is above and beyond, and I am forever grateful.

I would also like to thank our family friends, the residence and businesses for inspiring these seven short stories. It's never a dull moment.

Lastly, I would like to thank all of the students in the PWC program that I've had the pleasure of working with over the years.

# About the Author

Amber Shoebridge is in her graduating year completing a double major in Professional Writing and Communication, and History at the University of Toronto. She works at The University of Toronto Mississauga, and when she is not working, she indulges in her passion to write nonfictions stories about travel, history, family and food. Amber was first published in 2018-2019 edition of *Compass,* with the excerpt *"An Old Shoebox,"* from a family history story, *"Secrets of a House"*. She currently resides in the Greater Toronto Area with her husband Ron, and their two children, Lucas and Nicole.

www.ingramcontent.com/pod-product-compliance
Lightning Source LLC
Chambersburg PA
CBHW061731040426
42453CB00026B/912